Sears Hometown:

Modern Day

Indentured Servitude

By:

Richie

Johnson

Rickie Johnson

Sears Hometown:

Modern Day Servitude

ISBN-13: 978-1975844691

ISBN-10: 1975844696

Introduction

This book is about a once great company named Sears who created and spun off a company named Sears Hometown. That company Sears Hometown has developed a business system that equates to modern slavery or more accurate perhaps modern day indentured servitude. In this book we will look at the history of Sears Hometown and how it uses people to run their stores till they are run into bankruptcy. Then Sears Hometown steps in runs the stores till they resale them for a low price to unsuspecting people looking to try to find a way to make a better life. In reality they dangle the American dream of business ownership and providing a better life for their families to lure them into a business relationship that is completely one sided. The goal of this book is to keep good people from being deceived by the promise of free merchandise, a supportive company and the ability to be your own boss. The price of buying into their offering is deadly to the person and their families.

Chapter One
History of Sears Hometown

The history of Sears Hometown starts with its creator Sears, Roebuck and Co. so to fully understand how a great company went so wrong let us start with the history of the parent. In 1886, Richard Sears bought from Chicago watch retailer a shipment of watches/. The purchase changed the course of his life. The sales that he made from those watches launched a career as a watch retailer. Later, Sears hired watchmaker Alvah C. Roebuck to assist him. After some time working together, they decided to start a company by the name of Sears, Roebuck and Company. Sears after studying the retail habits of farmers in Chicago and the surrounding areas. That farmers paid high prices for products that were small and had high mark ups. His response was a mail-order catalog with a wide variety of products at clearly stated prices. The first catalog was produced in 1888, putting it in competition with Montgomery Ward's "Wish Book" that had been in circulation since 1883.

The Sears Roebuck catalog grew and swept the country by storm. By 1895, it has passed 500 pages' in size and sold almost any consumer product a working-class American family could desire. In later years, it sold automobiles and even kits for buildings, including churches.

In 1895, Julius Rosenwald purchased a half interest in the company and began to improve its management practices. When Richard Sears left the company in 1908 due to health, Rosenwald took over as president, in which capacity he remained until 1924. He remained as chairman until his death in 1932, when he was succeeded by his son, Lessing Rosenwald.

Sears adapted well to the growth of suburbs after WWII and crushed its ancient rival Montgomery

Ward. Throughout its history, Sears was noted for creatively adding to its list of consumer offerings, such as the addition of Allstate Insurance, which was sold at their retail stores.

Two decades after the end of the war, Sears completely dominated any listing of America's top retailers, but the seeds of its destruction were being sown by discount stores. Sears tried a variety of responses but was unable to maintain its position, and today is a company desperate to find a way to save its self. The company is closing stores and selling its well-known brands. It is selling its real estate and its even sold the Craftsman brand. It will eventually sell Kenmore and every other asset it has left in its balance sheet. Now Sears started a new journey as part of another failing American company. This company was named Kmart.

Kmart, home of the blue light special, bought the once-dominant Sears department store chain in a surprising $11 billion gamble. At the time they hoped to combine to compete against Wal-Mart and other big-box retailers.

This great farce was led by Kmart Holding Corp. chairman Edward Lampert, At the time of the merger it was hoped that most stores would survive, and several hundred stand-alone Kmart's throughout the country were to be transformed into Sears stores. The goal: A quick kick-start to sales away from Sears traditional base of shopping malls.

Lampert and Sears chairman and CEO Alan Lacy, when this was announced said the deal promised up to $500 million a year in savings within three years from store conversions, back-office job cuts, more efficient buying of goods and possible store closings.

Shares of both Kmart and Sears, Roebuck and Co. surged on the news, but some analysts were skeptical that it amounts to a home run. These analysts were correct. "Both have been broken in some sense," said Dan Hess, president and chief executive of Merchant Forecast, a New York-based independent research company. "Kmart has to learn to survive in a Wal-Mart world and Sears needs to learn to survive in a world of Home Depot and Lowe's.". This statement was the simple fact but no one in their management seemed to realize it.

Lampert at the time was 42, was as an assistant to Robert Rubin at Goldman Sachs & Co. before leaving to form a hedge fund at the age of 25. He orchestrated the deal and will has lead the company into ruin along with a board that dominated by Kmart directors. The Real Estate and other assets have been moved into position so that they can be liquidated to profit the hedge fund.

"We need to have a very low cost structure in order to compete with our biggest competitors," said Lampert, whose Greenwich, Conn.-based investment firm controls Kmart and is Sears largest individual shareholder, with a 15.8 percent stake. This statement points to what he and his managers came up to cut costs and run a retail operation where the managers would pay the costs for the company. That model is Sears Hometown.

For Sears, the merger allowed the company to move more quickly to where it believes its strongest base of customers are. "Off mall is where we need to move very aggressively," said Lacy, who became vice chairman and chief executive of Sears Holding. Lacy said he and Lampert have known each other for four years. The idea for a combined company first arose when they were in talks about Sears' purchase of 50 Kmart stores earlier this year, he said.

The new company was expected to have $55 billion in annual revenues and 3,500 outlets. That meant it only trailed Wal-Mart Stores Inc. and Home Depot Inc. among the biggest U.S. retailers.

It is headquartered in the northwestern Chicago suburb of Hoffman Estates, where Sears has its headquarters, but was to maintain a "significant presence" in Troy, Mich., where Kmart is based. This was not to become a reality. The one thing this merger saw grow was job loss and stores closures.

The deal was to be a remarkable comeback for Kmart, which filed for Chapter 11 bankruptcy protection in early 2002, leading to the closing of about 600 stores, termination of 57,000 Kmart employees and cancellation of company stock.

Lampert gained control of Kmart when the retailer emerged from bankruptcy in May 2003 through the conversion of his debt holdings into equity. Kmart had posted its first profitable quarter in three years.

While same-store sales had continued to decline, Lampert was said to have maximized cash flow in part by selling off some of the stores to Sears and Home Depot. Lampert said the goal for the combined company was to achieve a 10 percent operating profit margin, a level that's generated by such retailers as Gap Inc. and Target Inc. But he noted that in the meantime, the financial operations will be "lumpy" as it digests the two companies. Lumpy was to be one of the greatest understatements in history.

Sears Hometown Stores were established in 1993 as a franchise formula and Sears Home Appliance Showroom, established in 2007, offers primarily appliances. The stores are located away from shopping malls and small towns across the United States and several other countries. Sears Hometown Stores was spun-off along with Sears Outlet and Sears Appliance and Hardware in September 2012. Sears Holding is separating itself from all of the assets it plans to keep going after they close all of the large Sears and Kmart stores. They will let go of all of the employees and be left with a small work force. Most of their stores will be run and supposedly owned by hard working people. The rent, payroll and sales staff will be paid for by the small business owners who work their fingers to the bone for a dream that Sears hold out to people through smoking mirrors. Sears pays the owners less to cover all the expenses than what they paid their employees commission for sales. They make more per sale because the owners pay all the expenses. There are in essence indentured servants to the Sears master bound by contracts that are completely one sided.

Chapter Two

Own an established Sears Retail Store

in Your Local Town

The title is how they start their evil pitch to get you thinking of owning a Sears store and being part of their winning team. When in reality they are looking for a patsy to pay their rent, sell their merchandise, pay employee's that do their bidding and do all the work for less than they pay managers in their stores.

They usually offer some low price around $9,000 or maybe a little higher. They will finance the entire amount with no money down. Which it would seem is a great way to own a piece of an American icon. It seems like a way to build a future for your family. The person Once they make their pitch is caught up in a dream that quickly turns into a nightmare. The feel the person with the idea they will stand with them in the business. So the unsuspecting person enters into an agreement to run the Sears Hometown Store. An agreement that will require Sears to supply products that you do not have to pay for so it sounds great. Sears will pay a commission of up to 9% to you. One thing that becomes evident after you get into your store is that you rarely make 9% commission. You the business owner carries all the insurance on the products and pay all the expenses of owning a Sears Store. So you pay the rent on your building which usually sounds reasonable if you were receiving the commission they promised. But the rent becomes a cement brick around your neck. Sears can easily take this off of you by simply paying a few percent more in commission but they don't care. They will tell you to renegotiate your lease. They wait for you to fail then they simply take the store over and sell to another unsuspecting future bankrupt indentured servant. There are many other dangers of being a team member of Sears Hometown.

Chapter Three

The Sears Indentured Servant

Definition of Indentured servants were men and women who signed a contract (also known as an indenture or a covenant) by which they agreed to work for a certain number of years in exchange for food, clothing, and shelter.

Your store will be assigned a District manager who according to them is there to help you run the store. In reality they are there to keep spending your own money to run the Sears store. The money flows out of your pocket at an alarming rate. For example, when you sell a washer you may make 3% commission on the basic model. Which means at a price of $299 you make

$19 dollars. You have to unload it off their truck, then unpack it and put it on the sales floor. Then when it is sold you have to deliver it. If you are willing to work the store by yourself then perhaps you might make a small profit. But if you are like most people you have

to hire employees to do these functions. The commission does not cover your payroll costs. The payroll taxes will start to break your back because you are not paid enough by Sears. When you ask for help from the District Manager who supposedly is there to help you. You get told to cut down on payroll but make sure you have your store staffed at an expectable level. They don't care about your costs. During mower season it costs around 6 hours of labor to get one ready to sell. You have to take it of the truck then un pack it from a crate. Then you have to put it together then move it to the sells floor. When it is sold you have to deliver it. If a riding mower is $1,200 you might get 3% so a grand total of $36 dollars. Your payroll to get it sold is say $60 dollars. So you are paying out of your pocket to help Sears sell products.

Sears does have a bonus program which can help keep your business going. As of this book writings it is $5,000. It is based on several factors. Such as beating your last year's sales, having customer reviews, getting people to sign up for their credit services and meeting their new leasing goals.

If you check Sears history the stores year over year sells have been going down for the last 15 years. But a few stores are able to meet the totals and receive the $5,000. But even if you make the $5,000 bonus you District Manager can withhold part of it if you have in their opinion not met Sears goals in spirit. Many stores have their bonus withheld. Just like the indentured servant of old who worked hard chasing the goal of being free of the land owner. Sears Hometown always pushes their store owners harder to do more with less.

Chapter 4

The Store Owners are Great People in a Bad Situation

The victims of Sears Hometown the store owners are for the most part great people whose only flaw was being trapped by Sears in this web of deception.

The owners work hard to earn money for their families. They are over worked and constantly under stress. They want to help their customers and many really believe in Sears. They enjoy running their stores and do a wonderful job. Their dream of making money never is realized and most start to looking for a way out. Sears has you indentured for 5 years by way of a contract. They hope you will run their store for 5 years for free for them. Sears Hometown would have to pay much more if they ran these stores. In their stores the employees make 10% commission many times and have benefits. Plus, Sears would have to pay all the other overhead expenses. Like rent, insurance, maintenance and many more. The commission they pay in their stores is less than what they pay the employees so they have figured away with the Sears Hometown model to get sell merchandise for nothing more than the cost of the merchandise. Sadly, Sears cannot even make a profit by having indentured servants. A Sears Store owner does not get the 9% they promised but yet has to pay employees, taxes and other costs. They expect to run their owners into the ground so they might try to make money. If they treated their store owners with respect and paid a little higher commission they actually might make money. Because they would not have to constantly take over stores where the owners were forced into bankruptcy. They would have better sales people at the stores so they could sell more products. Their philosophy is to make money by mistreating their store owners. They want to make money by selling less each year which so far has not been a good concept.

Chapter 5

Sears Hometown Tricks

Sears Hometown tries to make themselves look good by announcing all kinds of new projects. One which sent many owners to the poor house was their new store look. This was called the A & E stores. This was supposed to increase sells by focusing on name brands instead of Sears brands. The cost of course was paid for by the store owner and they did not give you a choice if you wanted to keep making the much needed bonus. The complete new look cost way too much. They expected the stores employees and owner were expected to do the painting and other needed changes. No extra money was given for payroll to cover the

Sears Home Town: Modern day Indentured Servitude

massive increase in costs. The switch was sold as increasing revenue but in reality it was a way for the stores to market other brands because Sears is selling off its brands. They are selling Craftsman, Kenmore and the other brands. Now other stores will sell the Sears brands. Customers had to come to the Sears Hometown stores to exchange craftsman tools or purchase them. Many people love Kenmore and sears was the only place to purchase them. They have taken away the reason for customers to come to a Sears Hometown. Now Ace and other retailers who are in direct competition now carry the same products as the Sears Hometown stores. This makes a tough market even tougher. It is obvious to anyone who watches what Sears is doing that they are not planning to be around for much longer. They will try to get the store owners to keep working for free while the main Sears corporation sells off its assets.

Another trick of Sears Hometown is the promise of co-op advertising so you can advertise in your local market. The rules by which they require store owners to qualify for the program are difficult to do and time consuming. Your great boss the District Manager rarely approves it but is always trying to get you to advertise more. So you are stuck with the full amount for advertising.

Everything Sears does is a trick meant to get the owner to pay their cost. Sears Hometown wants its store owners to take merchandise back with no questions or replace it. But when you ship it back to them they often don't give you credit so you are out the money on the product. This alone can make a month go into the negative. But it is a great way for Sears Hometown to have a wonderful return policy for the public it is just not great for the store owners.

Another favorite way is to stick store owners is when a customer pays for delivery or installation. Sears often advertises free or reduced cost deliveries. When the product is delivered by usually third parties. They charge more money. Which is charged to the store.

So say a customer pays $75 for delivery the delivery team charges extra for hook up or because there were stairs. The extra charge many times is up to $100 more that comes directly out of the owner's monthly commission check. This can be a fatal blow when the owner might actually think they will make minimum wage that month after expenses.

Chapter Six

Invest in Another Sears Rip off Idea

One thing Sears is wonderful at is getting store owners who are working basically for free to invest more money to work even more for free. Sears has many other services it offers like carpet cleaning, selling carpet, kitchen refacing, roofs, windows and many more. You would think well this is Sears so after you buy a store you would be able to offer these services to make extra money-----WRONG!!!!! Sears will allow you to make money for them by offering these services but you must pay them money. Not just a fee covering say any training or display units but anywhere from $25,000 up depending on the service.

People invest in these services as an effort to allow their store to stay in business because most owners actually enjoy being Sears owners if they did not have to deal with Sears. These services in the end do not make the owners very much extra profit because just like the Hometown stores they have added costs hidden in everything that you sell for them.

Conclusion

Sears Hometown is a business model that resembles indentured servitude. It has been updated for the modern world. People who dream of living the American dream and are hard workers are suckered in to this concept. The people that own these stores are hardworking people who just want a better living for their families. They did not have a lot of money to invest and Sears Hometown was there to take advantage of them.

The numbers as you have read they are given in the beginning seem to be enough to make a profit so they purchase the store. It is not until they have risk e everything they realize that they have become unpaid servants of Sears. Sears takes every last dime they can extract from the owner till they discard them for a new owner and repeat the cycle.

My hopes in writing this short book is that people may be warned before they purchase a Sears Hometown store. I do not want any more hardworking people destroyed by this company. The founders of Sears would be ashamed of what their creation has become. It is even sadder that Sears cannot even make money when they getting their expenses paid by store owners. If you take away one thing from this book remember do not buy a Sears Hometown store.

www.ingramcontent.com/pod-product-compliance
Lightning Source LLC
Chambersburg PA
CBHW071203240526
45470CB00017B/1250